The Night of the Mary Kay Commandos

BLOOM COUNTY BOOKS BY BERKE BREATHED

The Night of the Mary Kay Commandos

BERKE BREATHED

A BLOOM COUNTY BOOK

Featuring Smell-O-Toons

LITTLE, BROWN AND COMPANY · BOSTON · TORONTO · LONDON

FIRST EDITION

Bloom County is syndicated by
The Washington Post Writers Group

The lyrics to ''Louie Louie,'' by Richard Berry, Copyright © 1957,
renewed 1985 by Limax Music Inc. and American Berry Music,
are reprinted by permission.

Library of Congress Cataloging-in-Publication Data

Breathed, Berke.
    The night of the Mary Kay Commandos.

    Selections from the author's comic strip Bloom County.
    I. Title.
PN6728.B57N5   1989   741.5'973   89-12228
ISBN 0-316-10738-7

10 9 8 7 6 5 4 3 2 1

Designed by Jeanne Abboud

WAK
Published simultaneously in Canada
by Little, Brown & Company (Canada) Limited

PRINTED IN THE UNITED STATES OF AMERICA

Critic's Page

"What is Bloom County? What is the matter with me that I don't understand it?"

—Gregory Peck

Los Angeles
November 16, 1988

1

4

5

7

11

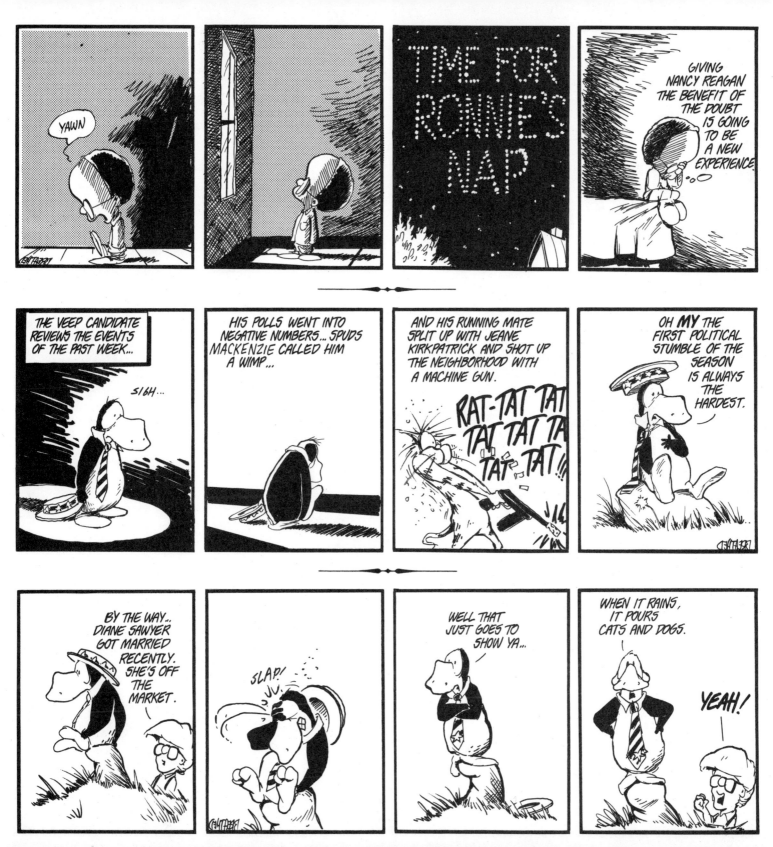

13

17

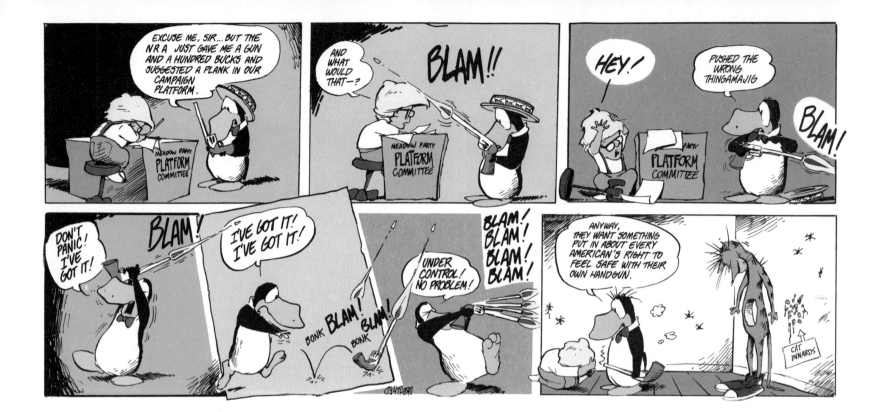

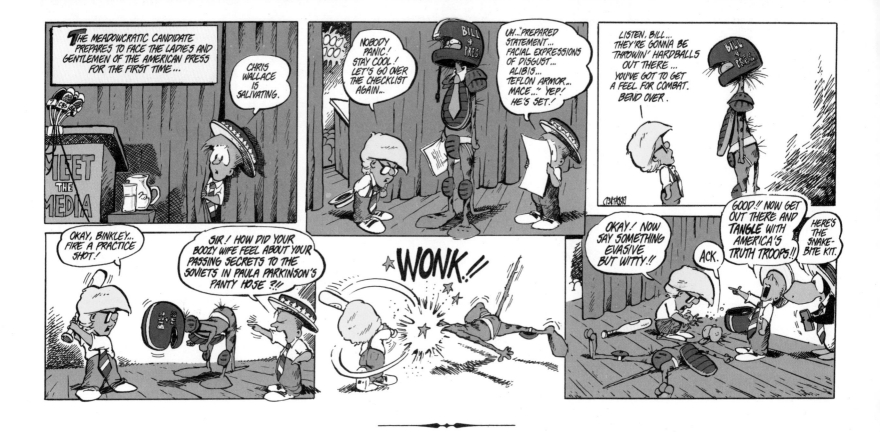

24

25

27

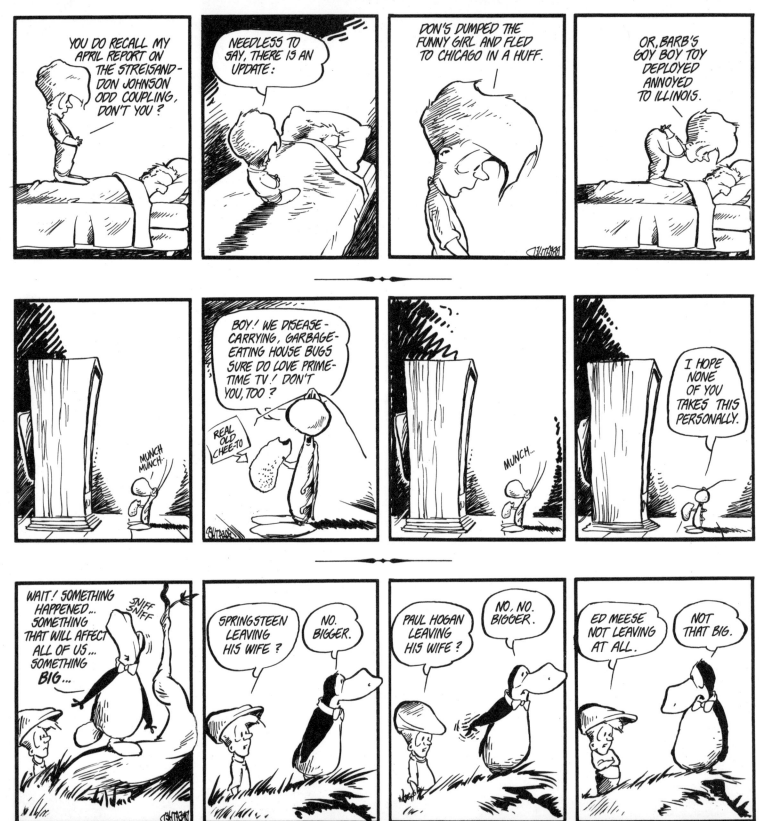

29

32

34

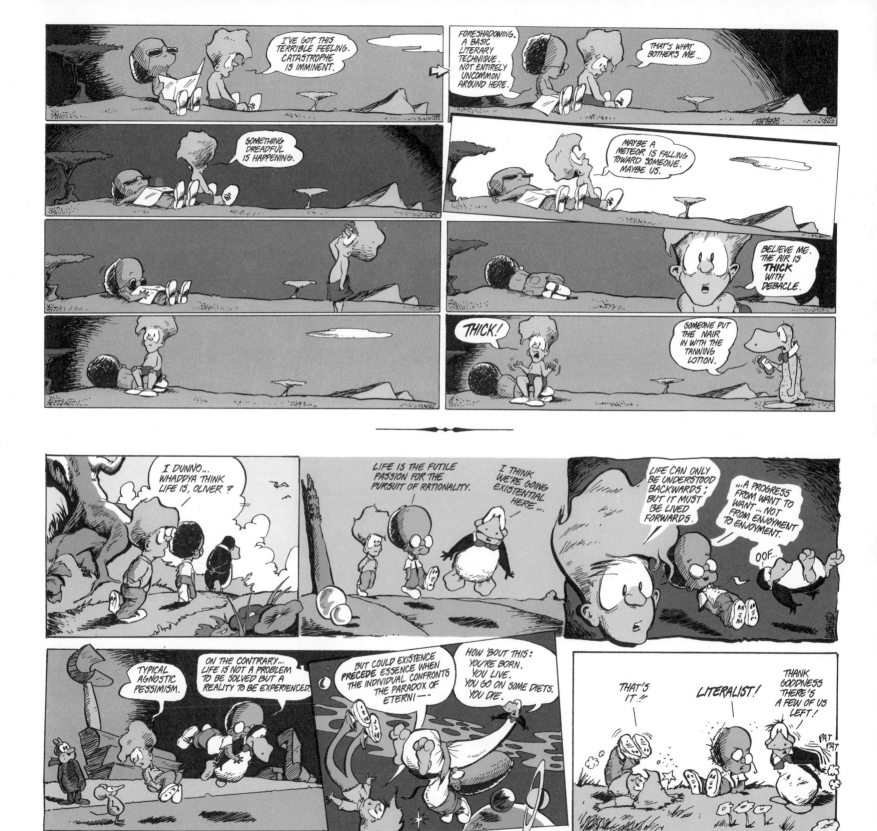

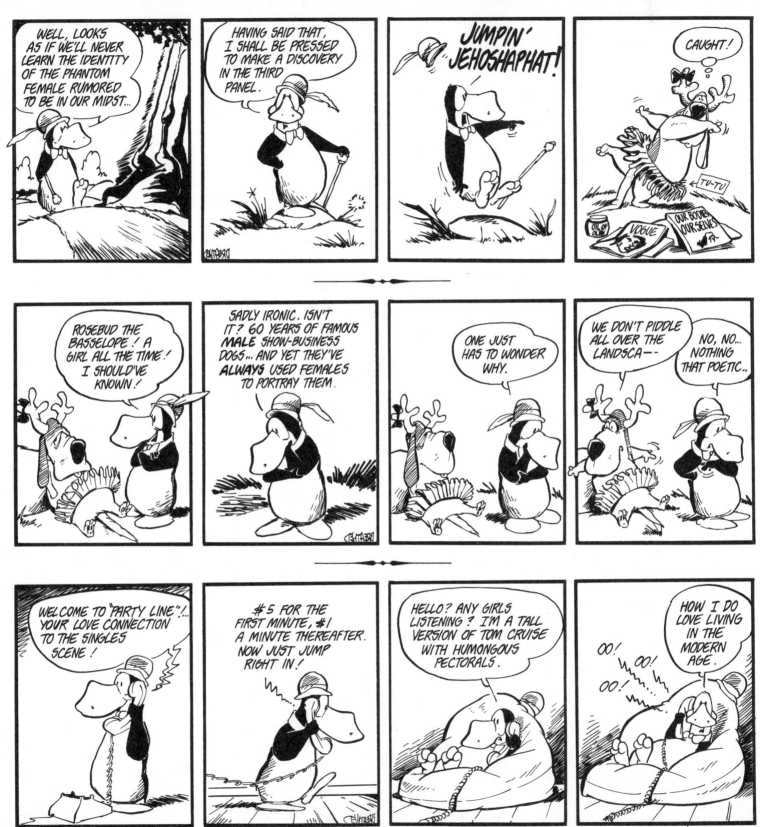

43

45

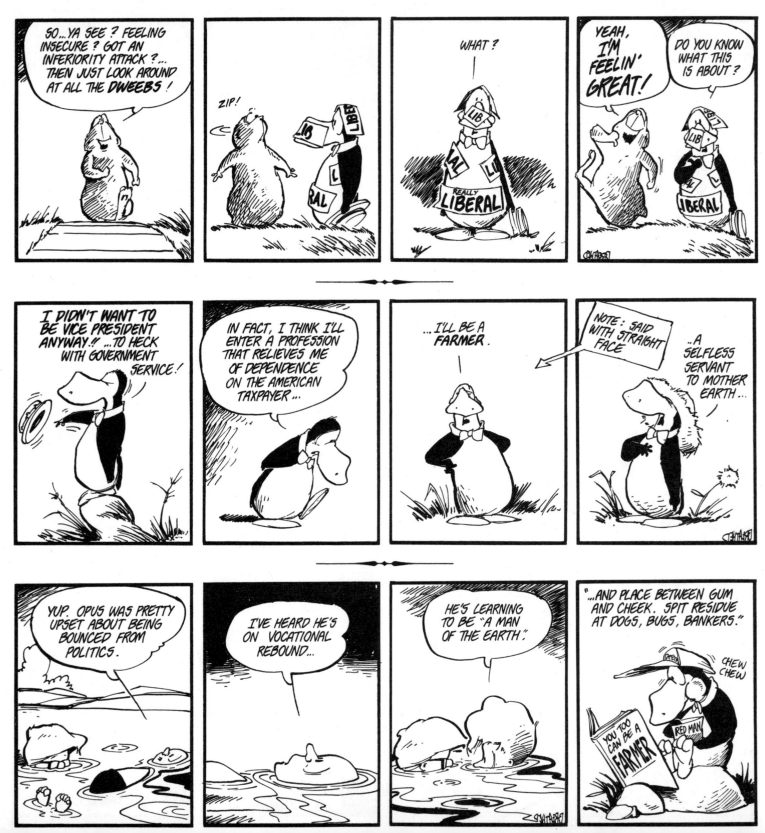

48

52

53

55

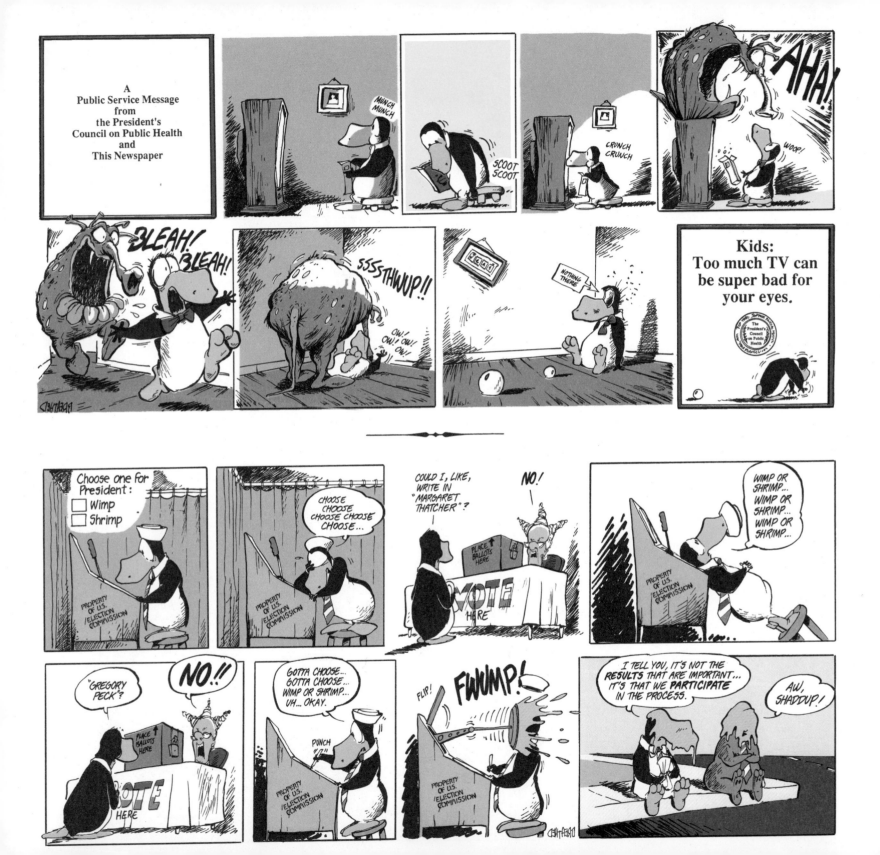

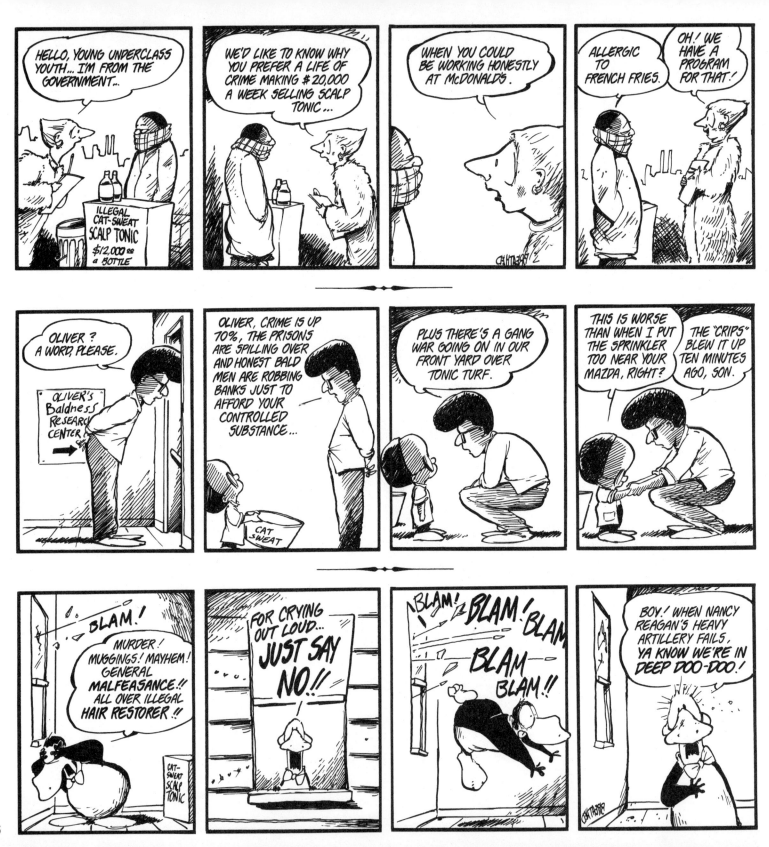

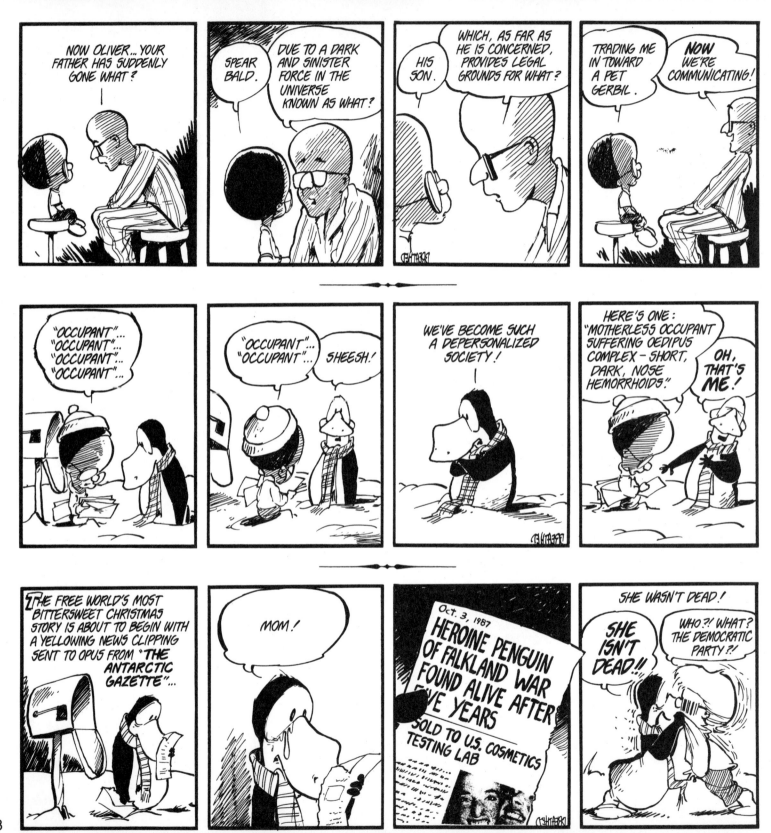

68

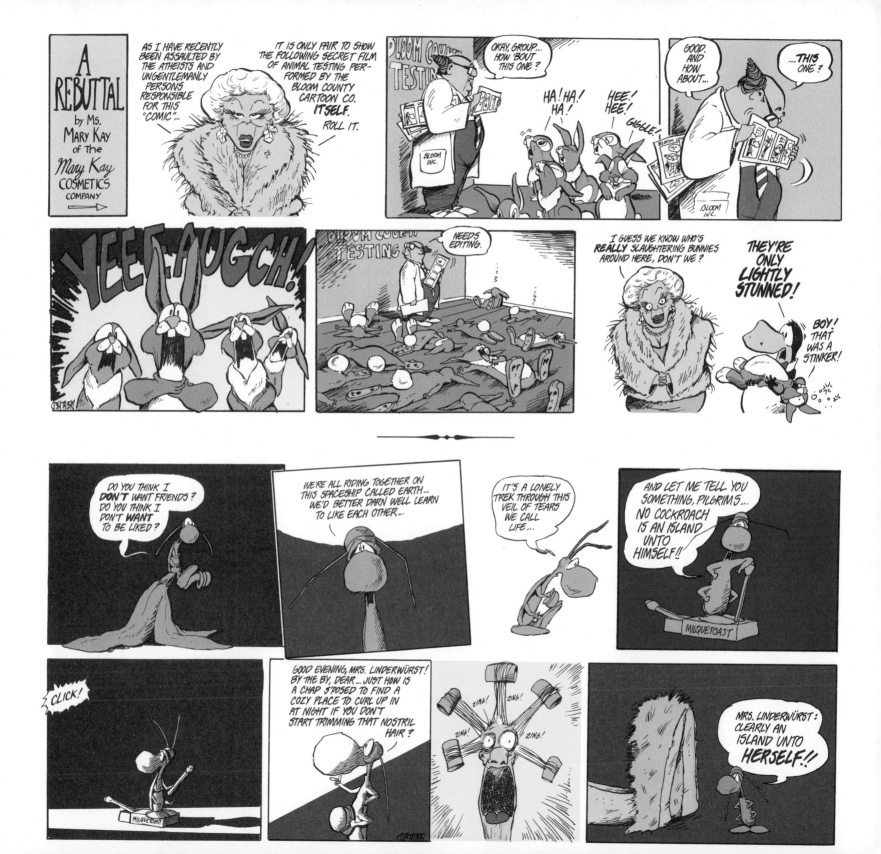

81

83